# 12 DAILY REMINDERS

Padmaraj Nidagundi

Copyright © 2021 Padmaraj Nidagundi

All rights reserved.

# DEDICATION

If you have ever thought to yourself, "I cannot change my life" this book is for you. In it, the author outlined: "Opinions don't define your reality, Everyone's journey is different, Things always get better with time, Judgements are a confession of character, Overthinking will lead to sadness, Happiness is found within and so on. This book provides a framework for how to change your life.

This book describes how you can make changes in your life and improve skills with 12 daily reminders. This book is about how to develop the skills to think positive every day.

In the book, the author comes up with some important themes:

The past cannot be changed.
Opinions don't define your reality.
Everyone's journey is different.
Things always get better with time.
Judgements are a confession of character.
Overthinking will lead to sadness.
Happiness is found within.
Positive thoughts create positive things.
Kindness is free.
You only fail if you quit.
What goes around comes around.
Smiles are contagious.

The author's idea is to share his own experience with this book about 12 daily reminders.

## 12 DAILY REMINDERS

## CONTENTS

1. The past cannot be changed ............................................. 1
2. Opinions Don't Define Your Reality ............................. 3
3. Everyone's journey is different ..................................... 5
4. Things always get better with time ............................ 6
5. Judgements are a confession of character ................ 9
6. Overthinking will lead to sadness ............................. 10
7. Happiness is found within ........................................... 12
8. Positive thoughts create positive things ................. 13
9. Kindness is free ............................................................. 16
10. You only fail if you quit ............................................. 19
11. What goes around comes around ........................... 21
12. Smiles are contagious ................................................ 23
Follow Along The Journey ................................................ 24

# 1. THE PAST CANNOT BE CHANGED

We all tend to think that the past has a lot of power over us. We grow up with family members that seem to act in ways that are not conducive to our well-being, and we carry those feelings into adulthood. We have friends who hurt us deeply and we experience a sense of abandonment that undermines our confidence in relationships with other people as adults.

And when those issues arise, there is often an impulse to want to go back in time and change what happened so we could somehow feel like ourselves again. But this is not possible. We cannot change the past, however much it might seem like we can fix everything if only given the chance.

Because the fact is, we are never going to get those chances. We are never going to be able to go back and change what happened. What happened is permanent. And even if it were possible to change something – for instance, if you found out there had been a mistake in your arrest or a mistake in the decision against you when you were charged with a crime – it would still not be possible to go back in time and undo the original event itself.

The past cannot be changed, which is an important

realization for everyone to come to terms with. You will never be able to change the past. It is not possible to change the past. And if you continue to try to do so, people will only reject you for it and your life will become more depressing and frustrating as a result.

Remember that the past cannot be changed and accept it as part of your present experience. As long as you keep these things in mind, you will have a better life overall.

Take care of your present.
Make your present an empowering experience.

Most people do not think they can control their present, no matter what. In fact, people with 5-year-old children seem to believe that because they have 5-year-olds, they cannot control their present. But this is not true at all. You have more power over your current than you realize. All you need to do is accept that everything has a path of its own and it is only by accepting it, by letting go, by trusting the universe that you will be able to take care of your present and allow it to empower your future.

Humans like to believe that time is linear, like a line of events leading from the past to the future. But that is not necessarily true. Because time can be seen as a path full of influences and opportunities, and we are all subject to these influences and opportunities. This means that you have some power over your present. If you want, you can change your present.

But what if the path to your present is a negative one? What if it was full of disappointment, sadness, fear, anger, and pain? What if those are the emotions that made up who you are today? It is quite possible – because we do not always have a choice in our influences. But through acceptance, by letting go of all these negative thoughts and feelings and letting yourself move forward with confidence without being burdened by the mistake's others made or the weaknesses they tried to instill in you, you can not only change your future but also shape it into something more empowering as well.

The past cannot be changed because it has already happened. Your past has already been taken care of by the universe, which means you will have to live with what happened no matter what you do.

## 2. OPINIONS DON'T DEFINE YOUR REALITY

Some people have opinions about you, but their opinion does not define how you feel. It is important to remember this when meeting new people, going on dates, and in your friendships. People form opinions about others based on what they know - and if someone doesn't know you well enough, they can only offer an opinion based on their experiences with other people in the past."

Your friends are your best guides who will tell you how your reality is being perceived by others. If someone has a negative opinion of you that is impacting the way they interact with or react to you, then it would be wise to spend some time getting closer to those friends so that they can guide you better.

It's easy to think that others know who you are and how they perceive you, but in reality, it is not true. If someone has never really known you, then it's possible that their opinion of you is based on them having an expectation of what they think a person like you should be like.

So, unless it is your opinion that your opinions define your personal experience, then you must take responsibility for your real life.

For example, if there are people who think that the world is flat when the world is not flat, then it could not be real. If someone's opinion is that you are a bad person, but this is not your opinion about yourself, then you know that it isn't true. If they are wrong about you and how they perceive you, then there would be a conflict between their perception of reality and your own personal experience.

Therefore, these opinions of others should not be part of your reality. It is the same for people who are in a bad mood, unhappy and have unrealistic expectations about relationships. If you related to their opinion, then it might look like there is something wrong with you. This is a very clear case of how what they think about you does not define your reality.

It is possible that others know certain things about you that are not positive and may hurt you. For example, if they tell other people that there is something wrong with you or say negative things to them about you behind your back, this can affect how others perceive you. However, it is not your fault, and you shouldn't take responsibility for their opinions.

Reality is not always affected by the opinions of others. It is possible that someone loves you, but another person doesn't even know you or like you. The truth is, they can never really know you unless they know you and see how reality has been affecting your life.

So, if someone says things about who you are that is not necessarily true or can be perceived negatively by others, it is important to remember that this does not define your reality - it is only their opinion of who they think you are.

## 3. EVERYONE'S JOURNEY IS DIFFERENT

No one can reach the peak in one day. It takes time. Everyone takes his or her own time to find out what path they need to take to reach their destination. Sometimes your path may be blocked. You may think, "I can't move forward anymore." Everyone has thought that before.

But, the path doesn't end there. You find a new place to start again. Each person finds his or her own route to reach their destination. Some people climb over some mountains and get on with their journey. Some people walk around the mountain and go to the other side of it. Some people use a packhorse to get around. Some people use a bike. Some people ride in a wobbly cart. You set yourself up somewhere else again and start your journey anew.

At the end, you have reached your destination. You may think that you have done very well indeed! But, it's only because you started from somewhere else and went beyond where you were at the beginning: that's why it seems like a "success". But, no one has ever reached their destination in one day. It takes time. It's only because people start from somewhere else and go beyond where they were at the beginning that they are able to reach their destination.

People who have become successful in one day, maybe those who have started from nowhere. But, there are very few of those people who can become successful in one day. Most people, including I, have been somewhere before and had to start anew to get where we're now. Many people still remain on their journey.

Why everyone's journey is different? For every single one of us, it has been the same feeling: that we have to reach our destination. At times like this, you may feel like giving up. But you do not have to give up just because of a little obstacle. Everyone's journey is different so there are many different routes each person takes in life. One thing is common though: everyone's journey has been a struggle, but it is worth it in the end.
So, where is your destination? What is the path to get there? Well, the only way to find out is to start walking.

So, let's begin our journey down that path together! So, what are you waiting for? Let's start your journey already! Remember, the destination of every person is different and the journey towards those destinations taken by each person is different. So, just believe in yourself. Everyone has seen you here and will continue to see you trying your best. Thank you for your attention.

## 4. THINGS ALWAYS GET BETTER WITH TIME

Time really does heal all wounds. It is hard to believe that after a period, a broken heart, or loss can simply turn itself around and turn into something happier. However, it is unfortunately true. The sooner we face the reality of the situation and accept things for what they are — that is when we move on and grow as individuals. We accept the change because it is inevitable to happen at some point in our life, but we also know that there will be a cure for whatever is bothering us eventually.

It is hard to believe that after a period, a broken heart, or loss can simply turn itself around and turn into something happier. However, it is unfortunately true. The sooner we face the reality of the situation and accept things for what they are — that is when we move on and grow as individuals. We accept the change because it is inevitable to happen at some point in our life, but we also know that there will be a cure for whatever is bothering us eventually.

So, think about something you're dealing with right now, the breakup of a relationship or break-up with your old friends. Think about why you are sad and how you feel now compared to how you felt at first. If you are feeling even a little bit better about the situation, then that is a good sign. If you're taking action and doing things to help yourself, feel better over time, time will begin to work in your favor.

And take note: if you are not feeling better about it after thinking about it objectively, then something else could be at hand. If you are still not feeling better after that point, then I would suggest asking for help — whether it be talking to someone personally or by reading a book on the subject — whatever helps.

**Remember your own mind is the battleground that determines whether you will be successful.**

Remember your own mind is the battleground that determines whether you will be successful. To counteract these negative thoughts, I like to try and say positive affirmations to myself (e.g., "I do the most productive thing at any given moment").

Take note: your subconscious is always analyzing what you are saying and doing. It is a phenomenal tool that will only get better with age, especially when you realize that many people do not even consciously know how to control their own emotions or make positive changes in their own minds! So, to become more aware of your own thoughts, I suggest practicing meditation.

**Meditation** is the practice of concentrating on one thing for an extended period. The goal is to find inner peace and clarity, which are crucial in restoring our "good vibe".

What does meditation have to do with positivity? Well, it is very important! My best friend from college started meditating and it changed her life around in a huge way. She used to be a bit of an angry personality that took whatever she wanted and did not mind being a little rude when she needed to be. But after two years of regular meditation sessions (every morning), she developed the ability to control her emotions and become more mature in general.

So, meditation is a tool that is very useful in helping us to become happier and at peace with ourselves. However, I also suggest using its applications on a daily basis so that you get the maximum benefit from it. Here is why:

If you practice meditation for 15-20 minutes each day, you will notice a great change in your general outlook on life. It will unplug you from the noise of the world around you and allow you to get into your own inner world where good things happen. This inner world includes all the important decisions and things that we can do to make our lives more positive.

**Focusing on the things that are positive.** You bring lots of positive energy into your life if you make an effort to focus on the things that are positive. For example, this could include:

**Happiness with friends or a new relationship.** My sister made me realize how great it is to be happy with your friends again, especially when you're really excited about spending time with someone. I wasn't like this in the past and didn't do anything to help myself; we all have a tendency to get stuck in our own ways, but if you change this it can make a huge difference!

**Learning something new.** With age comes wisdom and understanding (in my opinion). I'm always happy when I start learning something new and think about how it will help me in the future.

**Achieving a longstanding goal.** I'm sure many of you have a goal that's been in your mind for some time that you'd like to achieve. It's great to finally be able to achieve some of these goals, which will help you become more positive towards yourself!

**Best Strategy:** Think back on things that make you happy and just think about how great it is to be able to feel this way! When we are focused on the negative things, it's very easy for us to forget all about the positive things in the world — which are definitely worth celebrating!

**Positive people around you.** I like to spend time with positive people because they will remind me to be positive. The first step is to look for the good in a person and let that person inspire you, rather than focusing on their faults.

I have always loved watching funny movies with friends because they get me laughing and make the time go by so quickly!

**I believe in acting** (rather than sitting around), because I believe in things always get better with time.

# 5. JUDGEMENTS ARE A CONFESSION OF CHARACTER

You might be surprised to learn about who you are and how others perceive you. If you are curious about how others perceive your character and would like to see who is judging you. In the modern internet era, all you must do is jump on a social media site or type in your name in a search engine.

Or, if you are feeling less adventurous, look at the last time someone judged you and how they reacted when they really got to know the real side of who you are. These people who judge you already know about your wounds and weaknesses and still believe that they are qualified to judge your character. If they are friends with you, it is much more than enough for them to call themselves judgmental.

You can be really surprised how people are truly horrible and cruel to the ones they love. They are short-sighted and inconsiderate of the pain you might be feeling. The perception that others have of you is not necessarily true. You have a lot of things that you are hiding and being judged about. You are fighting battles that you cannot with anyone else but yourself.

Be careful of those who judge you because it's

possible that they're not saying it to be evil or even just because they want to bring you down, but they might be doing it out of a subconscious desire to be your hero. If they have the strength to see your weakness in a negative way, then maybe you should reconsider the good qualities that they see in you as well.

**Never take a person's opinion of you as fact.** Even if they consider you a good friend, it is okay to have weaknesses and flaws in your character. It's okay and expected that you will screw up at times. The real question is: Are you going to learn from these mistakes or keep making them repeatedly?

It is not about being perfect; it's about humanity. Be yourself and just be more compassionate toward others by recognizing their own flaws as well.

## 6. OVERTHINKING WILL LEAD TO SADNESS

Overthinking is a symptom of anxiety and depression that can make you feel terrible. As much as it might be helpful to think about things, going over, and over them again may just lead to despair. Some may argue that overthinking is healthy to prepare, and this time, it does. But remaining focused on what might happen is not always the best thing for you. It can become overwhelming and cause needless distress. The key to feeling peaceful again is taking control of your thoughts rather than letting them rule your life with fear-based thoughts or worries about what could happen.

To take back control of your thoughts, you must eliminate any fears from your life that are not warranted by reality (i.e., you can't predict the future). Eliminating fear from your life is a key part of making sure you do not overthink. Worrying about what might happen if something goes wrong in your life will do nothing for you except make you more stressed out. It's much easier to let go of anxiety-based thinking when we are no longer afraid of what might happen or how it may turn out. So, to control your thoughts, eliminate any fears that are not based on reality.

Some fears are based on past experiences. We may overthink because we are afraid of the future because of how something turned out the last time we tried it. The key to making sure you do not overthink is to not let yourself get caught up in these unhealthy thought patterns. When you think about the past, ask yourself what you learned from it and how it can be applied more positively in your life now – but do not linger there. You cannot change the past, and if dwelling on it leads you to over think, you may not be able to stop at just thinking about it.

If you have a fear of something in the future because of what happened in the past, writing down the fear and then writing how that situation could be handled positively will help you gain control of your thoughts again. It is easy to become fearful when you anticipate a negative outcome in something because of something that happened in the past. In order to stop overthinking, you must get a handle on your thoughts about the future.

Next, let us talk about thoughts that lead us into a state of worry and fear. When we get caught up in our heads, which can happen quickly and be incredibly hard to control, it is easy to fall into thinking that what happens in the future might not go as well as we would like it to. Beginning to think about something in the future can cause you to worry about it, and this leads to fears that result in overthinking. In order to not get caught up in thoughts of the future, you must accept that what happens is out of your control. Worrying about the future is a form of overthinking that will make you anxious and less able to enjoy your life instead of stress you out, which is what makes it a bad habit.

## How to control overthinking:

1. Accept that what happens is out of your control. This step is extremely important because it starts you moving toward a habit of not overthinking, but rather of letting go and trusting that any outcome that may come will turn out well – simply because it is out of your control.

2. Avoid worry about the future and get yourself into a habit of being confident – something I have talked about here before.

3. Accept that worrying will not change the outcome of anything.

4. Focus on present thoughts instead of dwelling on something in the future.

5. Accept personal responsibility for your thoughts, actions and reactions to situations and circumstances.

Ask yourself "What can I do about this?" rather than "Why is this happening?"

Finally, it is important to note that we don't always want to overthink something, like if we're trying to solve a problem.

# 7. HAPPINESS IS FOUND WITHIN

We have all been told that happiness is found within. But when our external situation is going well, it might make it easier for us to choose happiness, but it is not the cause of it. The key to authentic happiness comes from making wise choices and choosing to be happy. Let us explore what this means in practice.

**How to be happy:** You are not happy because you have a lot of money, a lot of friends, a beautiful home or because you have the latest technology.

You are happy because you make wise choices and choose to be happy daily.

You choose to be generous with your time, energy and attention. You choose to make personal sacrifices for others. You choose to give up your own values for the sake of making other people's lives better. You learn to manage what you do have and realize how much more there is that you want in your life.

You choose not to allow your circumstances to determine how you feel.

**Authentic Happiness:** The lack of external things that make life seem good is the cause of unhappiness!

The perception that we are being deprived and unhappy in relation to externally more important things is actually a form of mental illness.

If you want authentic happiness, then you must stop seeking happiness outside your own life power. You can find it within yourself by making wise choices and choosing to be happy daily by cultivating a contented attitude. In this way, you will realize that what makes your life matter is what you do with it.

**Happiness is found within:** You could spend your life chasing the wrong things in the wrong way and still be unhappy. You could waste a lot of energy feeling bad about yourself and still not like who you are inside. It's more important to make wise choices and cultivate a contented attitude than to struggle to find happiness outside your own life power.

Remember happiness comes from what we do with our time, energy and attention.

# 8. POSITIVE THOUGHTS CREATE POSITIVE THINGS

Positive thoughts help you to have more positive feelings and outcomes in your life. There is plenty of research that shows how positive thinking has a transformative effect on people's lives. Not only that, but it also leads to increased productivity, better relationships, and healthier lifestyle habits. Most importantly though is that there is an exponential increase in the probability of success when you are positively focused on yourself, your work, or projects.

Every time you think about what you want for yourself or for your work, know that those thoughts are creating an effect on your life and on those around you. Remember that they affect all aspects of your life - physically, mentally, and emotionally. They also affect the environment around you. So the choice is yours – do you want to focus on the negative or focus on the positive?

## 1. Positive thoughts create positive things.

The Law of Attraction (LOA) states that what you focus your attention on will eventually dominate your life. For example, if you are constantly thinking about something that is negative, you will most likely come across more negative things in your life. But if you focus all your attention on something positive and use all of your resources to make this a reality, it is likely that you will experience a more positive outcome. For example, if the first thing you think about when you wake up every morning is about how tired and stressed you are, chances are that your day will start off with a negative feeling. The same goes if the last thing you think about before going to sleep is all the things that went wrong during the day. It is just too much negativity. But, if you think about how wonderful your day was and how grateful you are for all the things that have happened to you, the chances are that your evening will be much more positive. Those positive thoughts are creating positive things in your life.

## 2. Gaining more confidence through realizing the power of positive thinking

Your mind is always searching out new things to see, hear, and experience. The number one thing it does is look at our lives as a journey and see where we need to improve from an emotional perspective. When we use our resources to focus on the positive side of things, we feel happier and more confident. We think more positively about ourselves, which is what gives us that confidence. However, when we focus on the negative, that is exactly what we are doing, and then we start thinking negatively about ourselves. It can be quite a vicious cycle sometimes because those negative thoughts create negative things in our lives.

When we are confident in ourselves, it is much easier to make positive changes in our lives. The Law of Attraction (LOA) states that what you focus your attention on will eventually dominate your life.

For example, if you are constantly thinking about something that is negative, you will most likely come across more negative things in your life. But if you focus all your attention on something positive and use all your resources to make this a reality, it is likely that you will experience a more positive outcome.

For example, if the first thing you think about when you wake up every morning is about how tired and stressed you are, chances are that your day will start off with a negative feeling. The same goes if the last thing you think about before going to sleep is all the things that went wrong during the day. It's just too much negativity. But, if you think about how wonderful your day was and how grateful you are for all the things that have happened to you, the chances are that your evening will be much more positive.

A simple mission, a few tricks, and positive thinking can transform your life. That is what three-time New York Times bestselling author of The Secret, Rhonda Byrne discovered when she decided to undertake an experiment to test the power of thoughts.

The first thing she did was pick a random person whom she had never met before and created a list of ten positive things about him or her. Byrne then spent three days writing down one positive thing about this person at the end of each day.

**In my life experience, positive thoughts create positive things.**

I will begin by talking about my personal experience. When I was 12 years old, my grandmother took me to see a doctor because I had numerous fevers and sore throats. At that time, I did not know that I had chronic tonsillitis. The doctor gave me some medicine to treat my condition, but it didn't help. Instead, my condition got even worse – I had a few fevers every week and was constantly laid up at home with a sore throat or just feeling sick.

I went to see another doctor and he told me that I needed surgery on my tonsils. He said they were very large and that this was the cause of the problem.

I started feeling a bit nervous, but I figured that the

doctor knew what he was talking about and that I had to trust him. So, a couple of days later, my mom brought me to the surgery clinic. I was so anxious! It was summertime and we were on our way to the mountains for vacation when I got called in for surgery. Later, we found out that this doctor in our town was really a quack. He started cutting holes in my throat with a saw and looking inside.

I started screaming as it hurt so much, but my mother just sat there and smiled at him – as if nothing were wrong! He asked me to open my mouth to check the inside of my throat. I could not do it without vomiting – then he got upset and said that I had tonsillitis! He gave me some medicine for the pain.

This was my first lesson in negative thoughts. This doctor was a charlatan. He just wanted to make money off me and had no interest in my health at all. And we trusted him! This is the best example of how negative thoughts can cause you harm. In this case, I had trust in a person that should not be trusted, and as a result, I suffered for two months feeling sick and in pain.

Later, I went to see another doctor for a **second opinion.**

## 12 DAILY REMINDERS

## 9. KINDNESS IS FREE

This is my experience with Kindness. It is about how kindness does not cost anything, but it can do wonders for the recipient. It can take somebody from hopeless to hopeful, and from fearful to free.

**Kindness is a gift that you give others as a way of receiving yourself.**

Today I am sharing with you little acts of kindness not only make the person receiving it, happy but also leaves a big positive impact on you.

### Give a compliment:

Have you ever felt down and out, and someone has complimented you on something that happened? But there is no way of you knowing when this compliment was given. Learn to give a compliment to other people, since it gives you a good feeling too.

You do not need to seek someone out for this, but if you are in a public place like the office or at school, compliment someone on their work. Think positive about them and say the words that come to mind. You can start by simply saying "thank you" when someone does something nice for you.

Be there for somebody who needs somebody to listen to their problems when they feel no one cares about them.

## Removing stones from Paths:

Have you ever walked and stumbled on a stone? It's very irritating because all you want to do is walk, but then you trip. This happens because we don't pick our path carefully.

Be a friend to those who have been thrown stones by somebody else. Be a bridge for them when they need one most and help them remove the stones that hinder their progress in life. Make sure they get picked up on the path that is fit for them and helps them achieve their desires in life.

## Standing Up for The Right Cause:

Have you ever noticed that a small voice inside you tells you to act? You want to do something about something that you feel is wrong. I am talking about the big things in life here like animal cruelty or child abuse. I am not talking about anything petty here. Be the voice of a child who needs help from adults or be the voice for an animal that cannot speak.

Are you being treated with genuine kindness and respect at home or at school? Or have you ever made a difference by standing up for the right cause in your life? Do something to make somebody else happy today and do it for free.

## Doing Good Things Without Expecting a Reward:

Have you ever thought of doing something good for other people without asking for anything in return? Do a random act of kindness today without expecting anything in return. Become the person who gives without expecting anything back.

Act of kindness can be as simple as calling another person a sweetheart because that is what they are or dropping off a hand basket of food at an elderly person's house or picking up their groceries from the supermarket. It does not have to be big things. It could be small things that you do for other people without expecting anything in return.

By practicing kindness, you will become calmer and levelheaded than before. You will start to see people differently, and you will become a better person yourself too.

Go on, do something good today without expecting a

reward. It is free, so you are guaranteed to get something good in return. If you, do it only once, then do not start bragging about it on social media. Let it be a starting point for your life changing journey to being a better person and see what good it can bring to your life.

**Being a Senior give advice and notes to your juniors.**

Being a Senior does not mean you have to be old. It means being someone who will be there to help others in need when they are at a disadvantage. Being kind, giving advice and notes to your juniors and to your seniors, is necessary in today's society where everybody needs a helping hand.

The older ones are capable of helping the younger ones with their problems if they will just step up to the challenge. But we cannot expect people to step up if it's not encouraged.

In today's society, the younger ones can easily take advantage of the older ones by using their kindness and advice for their own purposes. We shouldn't let them do that but give them some encouragement to be kind to others and do this in a positive manner.

**Help a friend in doing assignment.**

You are working hard for an exam, and you are desperate to pass. There is nothing better than having a friend who will help you do your homework assignments, because you are too nervous to do so.

You need to be someone who is ready to help others when they need it. You have to encourage your friends; and when they ask you for help, then don't hesitate for one moment in giving it as much support as possible for them.

After you help them, they are sure to give you the same support when you need it. This is how we all should work together for each other for the same purpose.

Not there to get something in return but to do something good for others without expecting anything back from them.

## Be a Guide.

Do you know what it is like to be lost? Have you ever been lost in a place that you don't know, and have no idea how to get back home. It is very scary sometimes, because we always think of ways to get out of it.

It is the same thing when you lose direction in life. You feel very lost because you do not know what will happen next if things continue like this for a while. This is how your future looks if things continue this way.

You have to be a guide for others and for yourself. By staying positive, things will work out for the best. Being optimistic is a great way to lead your life and make the most out of it.

When you are positive about things, then you will see the brighter side of life. You will see that there is a way out when you think there is not one. You will become a light in the darkness because you are not afraid of taking up challenges anymore.

## 10. YOU ONLY FAIL IF YOU QUIT

No matter what you are doing, failure will never be the result of a lack of trying. The key to succeeding is not in your intelligence or talent, but in your persistence. So if you ever feel like giving up, remember: You only fail if you quit.

In my experience it is all about what it really means to succeed and how important persistence (not ability) is for achieving goals. I have seen it time and time again; people who quit because they feel like they don't have the necessary intelligence or talent.

### 1. You will fail if you keep giving up.

If you see a pattern of giving up when things become difficult, then you are more than likely doomed for failure. Someone who is destined for success will find a way to push through these challenges by figuring out what is causing them.

### 2. Success is about ability to persist.

Life is filled with difficulties; you will always have problems to solve and goals to achieve. It is how you deal with them that defines your success. The difference between those who succeed and those who fail are the ones who can persist through their challenges.

## 3. Don't let people convince you that you won't make it.

There are many different definitions of success and the one you choose for yourself should be the one that fits your dream. You will receive lots of negative feedback when you refuse to listen to excuses. Here is a good article that covers why excuses are only toxic to everyone else.

## 4. Don't give up no matter what others say!

"The phrase that I've come up with is, 'It is better to die trying than to live on your knees begging forgiveness. It is better to fail at something than to be a coward and be a failure. It is better to be a success than a coward." -Mark Victor Hansen

If your goal is important enough, you should not let others stop you from achieving it. You are the one who has control over your life; if you believe in yourself, then there is no way you can fail. Some people refuse to give up and their dreams come true because of this.

## 5. Winning starts with one step at a time.

This is how it works in most games: if you fail 10 times or so, you start over again from the beginning. If you do not keep trying to beat your record, then eventually the game will become unplayable, and you will be stuck playing for fun rather than trying to win.

## 6. Be persistent; never give up on a goal that is important to you.

I admire people who are persistent even when they know it will hurt them. They could quit and wonder why they did not get what they wanted, but instead they push on and keep trying. The same goes for all other goals in life; everyone has at least one big goal that is important to them.

## 7. Be confident in your dreams.

If you believe in yourself, then there is no way you can fail. It is amazing how you can change someone else's life just by believing in yourself.

## 8. Always have a dream and a purpose.

Personally, I have failed more times than I really care to admit in my life. But that does not mean I am going to give up on my dreams! You should never regret the goals you set for yourself because if your goals are important to you then there is no way you can fail.

## 9. Success is how you feel about yourself.

How you define success will be different for every person, but one thing is certain: You will not feel successful if you are not persistent with your goals. I have always liked the "Waste not, want not" saying because it fits with what I believe.

## 10. Success does not just happen; it is about working hard to achieve your goals.

There are many different ways to define success. The one that will be most important to you will always be the right one for your goals. Persistence is the key to success, so never give up on your dreams. If you can work hard then you will achieve your goals in life!

## 11. WHAT GOES AROUND COMES AROUND

What goes around comes around —or does it? If you know about karma, the answer is yes. Karma is one of the oldest and most universally acknowledged truths in the world. The word "karma" literally means "activity," and can be divided up into a few simple categories—good, bad, individual, and collective.

The practice of karma has been embraced by many cultures throughout history and its influence extends deep into the modern world. It is believed that karma affects our present lives, our past lives, and future lives and that every action we take will affect our future life. Indeed, the belief that bad behavior will eventually come back to haunt an individual is deeply entrenched in society today.

While karma is widely believed in, it is often misunderstood by the public. This is no surprise when you consider its core meaning—the effects of a person's actions on another person either in the past or present. The practice of karma takes many forms, but it can be summed up with one word: retribution.

The concept of retribution and karma stems from the Hindu and Jain religion and from pre-Buddhist religious practices all over the world. Karma refers to the idea that every action has an effect on the world and on subsequent actions of a person. Therefore, when a person behaves in an unkind way, he or she could expect retribution from others in their life—equal measures of kindness and respect received or deserved will be returned.

Karma is most often associated with justice. It means that when people commit crimes, they should be punished for their actions. On the other hand, if people avoid committing crimes, they should be rewarded for their actions.

Don't you hate when you receive a rude text from someone and all you want to do is call them an expletive, or when someone cuts in front of you in traffic and it takes everything in your power not to flip them the bird? You are not alone.

We all have moments where we want to vent with a good old-fashioned, passive-aggressive text or email — but that impulse is often best ignored. Because honestly, what goes around comes around. And frankly, that is an email you could live without.

So, the next time you are tempted to fire off a nasty message, take a deep breath and ask yourself: Is this going to make me feel better in the end?

Because while it may feel good now, you must ask yourself if the joy of sending that jibe is going to last. Because chances are it is not. Think about how much time you will spend fuming over the nasty message you just sent.

"If you fire off a mean email or text, you're going to regret it eventually," says career coach Penelope Trunk. "At that point, you've wasted all this time and energy being angry and writing a harsh note or email."

It is easier said than done, but just try to put aside your pride and think about the message the sender will get from your passive-aggressive emails. Most of the time the other person is not getting the message you intend.

## 12. SMILES ARE CONTAGIOUS

Smiles are contagious. This is due to the fact that our facial expressions like happiness, sadness and anger can have a significant impact on those around us. So, as the saying goes, "if you want to be loved, give love." Dozen of studies have been conducted on this topic including one done by Janet Surrey in 2008.

Surrey's study used a group of participants who were assigned a task to do. Each participant was asked to create an emoticon, which is what pop stars and other celebrities use for their social media posts. The emoticons ranged from neutral faces to smiles to frowns. Later, each participant was asked to show their face to the next person in line and that person was asked to draw the face they saw on the paper. The participants were told to not talk while this exercise was being done. The participants were then asked to describe the face they saw and each person concluded how they felt about the person they saw. This was repeated multiple times by each participant and a score was given on how accurate everyone that drew the face perceived it to be. Some people perceived smiles when there were none, while some drew a frown when there was no frown or sad face when the individual had no sad expression on their emoticon.

**Smile! It makes everyone in the room feel better!**

In conclusion, the study found that even though people did not smile or frown, they perceived each face to be as if it were smiling or frowning because each emoticon contained a facial expression that was different from the other emoticons. In addition, when people were asked to describe the faces drawn by their partners, they described the faces as being happy or sad even though they did not smile or frown.

This is because subconsciously we are always smiling and frowning. The emotions can be controlled by us subconsciously because our facial expressions can have a significant impact on those around us.

## FOLLOW ALONG THE JOURNEY

The author concludes this book. "This book is about 12 Daily Reminders, and it seeks to challenge the way we typically think about our daily life thinking. It attempts to shift how people view what makes their daily life thinking, to provide inspiration for a different kind of daily reminders."

This book is an opinion. It outlines a framework for life that provides a theoretical foundation, for action in the field of daily reminders. It attempts to shift how people view what makes their daily life thinking, to provide inspiration for a different kind of daily reminders.

This framework was developed by Dr. Padmaraj Nidagundi and the author with repeated use over the last ten years.

The author invites those who share this thought process to consider this book as an invitation to participate in developing and using this framework in their own lives. This book is for those who are looking to use daily reminders as a tool to enable them to live a more meaningful life, where their daily thoughts and actions create the desired results.

The author shares his experience on how this process has helped him in his personal life and his work. By using this framework, a person will be empowered with the ability to make new choices. He will be able to take control of his life by exploring new possibilities that could have otherwise remained hidden.

This book is useful for those who want to be empowered and for those who will guide their organizations. It will be useful for those who are seeking to develop a framework to create an organizational culture that creates a breakthrough in the performance of its employees.

## 12 DAILY REMINDERS

Before I finish reading this book! Let us make some notes to follow up:

Why I need daily reminders?
_____
_____
_____
_____

Why my past cannot be changed?
_____
_____
_____
_____

Why opinions Don't Define Your Reality?
_____
_____
_____
_____

Why everyone's journey is different
_____
_____
_____
_____

# 12 DAILY REMINDERS

Why my past cannot be changed

Why and how things always get better with time

Why judgements are a confession of character

Why I need to stop Overthinking

# 12 DAILY REMINDERS

How to be found happiness within ourself

Why kindness is free

How positive thoughts create positive things

Real meaning of You only fails if you quit – in my life

# 12 DAILY REMINDERS

Why smiles are contagious

To 10 take away from this book

## 12 DAILY REMINDERS

# ABOUT THE AUTHOR

Padmaraj Nidagundi, the author of many books, works as an engineer, among other works, lives in Latvia, Riga, with his wife, Alina, and their one child. In this book, the author's goal is to bring his best collected 12 DAILY REMINDERS.

# 12 DAILY REMINDERS